Let's   Talk
About

By Zykia McCoy

Sex

the sum of the structural, functional, and behavioral characteristics of organisms that are involved in reproduction marked by the union of gametes and that distinguish males and females

Jazelle

There is something so intoxicating about tasting myself on my lovers lips. It sends jolts of electricity through me. He will always be sexy or otherwise he will never get a ticket to the show in my bedroom. Head is a must there is something to be said about a man who knows his way around a clit and Mr. Jerry Donovan sure knows his way up around down and through a va jay jay. I have been seeing Mr. Donovan for about four weeks now and tonight was his lucky night. He had finally passed the test to explore my fun zone. He wanted me to meet his family tonight but I choose to have some fun instead. "Jazelle I want you to meet my parents. We have been dating for some time now and I would like them to see who I have been talking about". I smiled and politely declined. "Jerry it has only been a few weeks. I don't want to ruin what we have going by rushing the family thing right away". Truth be told I had a few other situations in the works as we speak so getting serious with Jerry would complicate things too much. Even though Jerry was all the man any woman could ask for standing at six foot three , creamy chocolate skin and biceps on triceps with the most heart warming golden eye's you ever could see. I was a woman of many taste and didn't see a point in limiting myself to just one flavor. Rico and Barry both knew of my playmates and accepted the fact that they would never be the only man in my life but Jerry was sensitive and I found myself protecting him from his own feelings. Then there was Marshell the sweetest white boy you ever did meet with his ice blue eyes and pearly white smile. He and I worked together at my business firm I made the happy mistake of sleeping with him at my company christmas party. I say happy mistake because that white boy put it on me. Not only could he give head but his trunk size could match with the brothers any day. I , like most expected to see an average size man stick but he whipped out a vanilla flavored mandingo that had me almost running for the hills. He knew I would not settle either but that didn't stop him from stopping by my office everyday looking to entice me on getting down with the swirl again. I put him on ice for now. Trying to keep my lady dip between the three was going to be hard enough. Especially since I added Jerry to the mix I find myself preoccupied, besides we work together and I love my job I would not want to complicate things to the point where I could not enjoy my work environment. As Jerry's tongue leaves a trail of me on my lips I am snapped back into reality while he leaves a trail down my body. All the way down to my toes. One by one he licks and sucks and I have to say I have never had a man who liked feet enough to put mine in his mouth but for some reason it turned me on even more. I could no longer take it I sat straight up in the middle of the bed and took Jerry's 11 inch monster into my mouth and inhaled as much of him into the back of my throat and slurped and sucked like a porn star until he began to moan and caress my hair. " Oh Jazzelle, don't stop". I love it when they say my name. Now I am no expert but I definitely know my way around a dick and i'm not shy with my skills. Once Jerry felt he would explode he eased my head off his head and looked me deep into my eyes "turn over". I complied giving him back control of the situation. I tooted my ass high in the air with anticipation of penetration. With a swat at my cheek Jerry said in a husky voice "huh hun lay flat on your stomach". A bit perplexed but intrigued I complied. Excitement building up caused me to leave a little puddle under me. I felt the weight of Jerry's dick smack each ass cheek. Jerry leaned right down into my ear "This is what you want" smack. "Yes daddy" I replied a little above a whisper. He took two fingers and stroked them in and out of my mouth. Smack with his dick. I have never reached this height of arousal without penetration. "I can't hear you jazelle is this what you want". Smack. "Yes daddy" I say a little louder. He sticks his fingers in my mouth again this time spreading them so he can see my tongue. I nut a bit more onto the covers making the puddle bigger under me. Jerry slides his dick over my clit toying with me. "You want me to fuck you Jazelle". "Mmmhum yes please". I can feel another nut coming on and I try to grind on his member but he puts his hand on the small of my back forcing me back down on the bed. "Not yet, you're not ready for him". He bends down and begins to trail my back with kisses giving me goosebumps all the way down when he gets to my ass he kiss each cheek. Then without warning he snatches my legs open and dives face first into my asshole. I have never had any man explore me like this. At first he licked the hole then he stiffened his tongue and fucked me with it. I never knew I would like anal but Jerry proved me wrong. He started by taking the same two fingers that he put in my mouth into my pussy while he tongue fucked my ass. I thought I would pass out from the orgasms then when I thought I was done Jerry took one finger and slid it in my ass I lost control and began to convulse. "Oh My god". Was all I could get out. Jerry made sure I didn't forget him. I felt tingles in places I never knew could tingle. After taking my anal virginity for a while Jerry eased himself into my pussy which was wetter than niagra falls at this point. With my eyes rolling back into my head my body vibrates under his command. I couldn't breathe , think , move or utter a word. With each stroke he gave me another inch and then another. Until he had me climbing the walls trying to run from the dick. Once he had reached his peak I tried to suck him dry. I caught every seed that left his body and turned the tables and had him running from me. As we lay in the preparation of our escapades I began to think how well Jerry put it down. He definitely left his mark. "I would like to applaud you on a job well done" I said huskily. I heard Jerry chuckle "You know I will do whatever it takes to please you".There it was the sensitive emotional side of Jerry that I fought hard to protect. Now that I had the chance to experience what treats were in his bag I definitely needed to make sure I kept him happy. The next morning I was awaken to a pleasant surprise, Jerry face deep in my pussy. He was really trying to make me fall in love. After drinking me all up Jerry planted a wet nasty kiss on my lips I began reaching for his man stick but he pulled away. "No baby I need to go to work just wanted to make sure you were taken care of". Jerry continued to win points. I settled in for a nap and enjoy my day off. My phone filled with messages woke me up and it seemed like I only got about ten minutes of sleep. Most of my messages were from Rico telling me he needed to see me soon for a fix. After the hurting Jerry put on me there was no way in this world I could even entertain the thought of tangling with Rico right now. Barry text me inquiring about when the next time we could hook up. I would have to speak with them on a later date the message that caught my eye the most came from my office. "Hey Jazelle it's Marshell, I hate to interrupt your day off but Trish is looking for the Robinson file. She needs you to come in and find it as soon as possible thanks". That was just great, I planned on a relaxing day lazing around the house, so much for that. Getting up I began to get dressed when it dawned on me why would Marshall be calling me instead of my boss Trish. This was a set up and I was glad I smelled it a mile away. Calling Trish I had so many thoughts racing through my brain. "Hi Trish I left the Robinson file on your desk before I left yesterday". "I know Jazelle I have it completed already. Are you feeling ok". Here I was looking like an idiot "Yeah I am fine I was just making sure you received the files you need. See you tomorrow". Shaking my head I decided to go down and get some breakfast being that it didn't look like I would get any sleep. I figured I would stop by the office after eating to get to the bottom of this stunt Marshall tried to pull. Pulling into the parking lot of Le Bistro my phone began to go off before I could get out the car. Irritation took over my body but quickly faded when Jerry's name popped up on the screen. "Hello Sir" I cooed into the phone. "How is the most beautiful woman on earth feeling. I didn't wake you did I?". I could not stop smiling "no I am getting breakfast, how's work going". "It's going. I wanted to lock you down for dinner plans this evening and it sounds like I can grab you for breakfast this morning". "Jerry I told you I am out getting breakfast already". He chuckled "maybe one day i'll get you to offer to do something nice for me. How about you pick up Breakfast for the two of us and come to the office and we can enjoy breakfast together". Normally I would have turned Jerry down flat but he had me feeling things I don't normally feel. I had butterflies in my stomach, this was crazy. Before I could stop myself I heard me saying "sure why not what would you like".

After getting our food I hurried to Jerry's office. I felt like a schoolgirl with her first boyfriend. It was crazy how a little sex could have me tripping like this. On my way to Jerry I received a text from Marshall telling me how urgently they needed me to come to the office and get these files. I simply text back i'll be there when I get there. Walking into Jerry's office I felt a little out of place. I had never been to his job before. Waking up to his receptionist I found myself being read before I could get any words out of my mouth. "The modeling agency is two buildings down". Caught off guard I quickly responded "excuse me". I wasn't sure if I should be flattered or offended. "Oh god you don't speak english" she began to reference with her hands leading me to the other building, offended. "Excuse me I am here to see Jerry Donovan" I stated with a little attitude. She looked me up and down and gave me attitude right back "I don't know what Mr. Donovan would want with someone like you". I took a step back and pulled out my phone "hey beautiful, are you on your way?". I took a deep breath before responding, "I am actually here and your very classy assistant has insulted me not once, not twice but three times". Before I could continue Jerry stormed out of his office with rage in his eyes. ""Pamela what has gotten into you?". Pamela's eyes were as big as saucers "Mr. Donovan I was just say..". "I don't give a damn what you were saying When you see this woman you better show her the utmost respect do I make myself clear". Pamela put her head down "yes sir". "Jazelle I apologize for Pamela's actions shall we". He took my hand and guided me into his office and I must say it turned me on for him to defend me like he did. Jerry pulled me in a in his arms and planted a sloppy wet kiss on my lips. His tongue felt amazing messaging mine, so amazing in fact I found myself moaning. "How about we get straight to dessert". Before I knew it Jerry had my legs spread wide over his desk while he feasted on me like I was his last meal. I couldn't help but to scream out "oh god Jerry". I found myself breaking another cardinal rule. I never screamed out a man's name during sex this makes them feel like they have all the power. As much as I hated to admit it Jerry was in complete control of my mind, body and emotions. After cleaning my juices off of Jerry's face I went to work on his hammer. I made sure he tickled my tonsils as I inhaled as much of him as I could. "Jazzelle i'm about to cum". I massaged his balls until I milked him of his man milk. I stood in front of him with a huge smile on my face as he shivered in his chair. "Where are your condoms?". He pointed to his bottom draw. I quickly retrieved the gold package and applied it to Jerry's tender member. As soon as the condom was secure I mounted his lap and ride that stallion until my legs gave out on me. I was very thankful for Jerry's private bathroom with a shower. After another round in the shower we washed each other and enjoyed our breakfast which had now become lunch. Sometime after eating I ended up dozing off on Jerry's couch. "Jazzelle, baby it's time to wake up". I was awoken by the sound of Jerry's voice. Looking out the window I could see the sun had gone down. I must have been much tireder than I thought. Jerry had worked me out and my body hadn't been worked like that in years. "What time is it?" I asked sitting up. Jerry smiled "dinner time". He chuckled. I gave him a look that said I actually wanted a time."it's 7:45. I made reservations for us at Shea Marie's for eight o'clock so I don't mean to rush but we have to go". I quickly slipped on my shoes and rushed out of the office to my car, which was no longer where I parked it. "I had it sent to your house, our car is waiting over here". Jerry yelled to me from a town car that I had overlooked in my rush. "Mr. Donovan you sure know how to treat a lady". I said sliding into the car. The food was superb I could not complain about anything. I smiled the entire night. "Jerry I would love for you to come over for a night cap but I think I need time to recuperate if you want me to look presentable for your parents this weekend. This put a huge smile on Jerry's face. "Jazelle you have made me the happiest man on the planet". Jerry said planting kisses all over me. "Ok Mr. paws off. Driver please drop Mr. Donovan off first". I giggled as Jerry continued to shower me with kisses. Pulling up at my place it was very hard for me to get out of the car and make my way to the door. I wanted Jerry to stay the night so bad but I really needed a break. Walking up to my dwelling I noticed a figure standing in the corner of my porch. I casually retrieved my mase and made my way to my door. I waved to Jerry and without looking sprayed the figure as Jerry pulled off I pulled out my phone and dialed 911 as the figure screamed. "Ahhh Jazelle it's me Barry". "Barry what the fuck are you doing at my house unannounced". While I yelled at Barry the operator reminded me I had called the police. "Ms. can you hear me where is your emergency?". Taking a deep breath to calm my voice I responded "I am fine it was an accident I apologize". "Mam are you sure you don't need emergency assistance?". I shook my head at Barry's pitiful self "yes i'm sure thank you". I quickly opened the door so el stupido could wash his eyes out, didn't want him to go blind. Come on here I took him to the kitchen and used the hose from my sink to rinse his eyes out. Once he could see and talk I wanted answers. "What are you doing here Barry?" this asshole had the nerve to smile and make a move toward me. "I came to see you baby". I quickly brushed him off. "Barry you know the rules , you don't show up at my house unannounced and you damn sure don't hide in the darkness". Barry had the nerve to suck his teeth "you have been ignoring me all day and now I know you ain't read none of my text or listen to my voicemail because I told you I was coming to get some of that late night action". He advanced me again this time I side stepped him "Barry there are rules for a reason. You knew what this was and you agreed to it now you're acting brand new". "I know what it is that's why i'm here. I'm horny as fuck and besides rules change". He advanced me again this time grabbing hold of my wrist "Barry let me go. I am not fucking you tonight". He ignored me as I struggled to release myself from his grasp. "You feel that big dick, he ready to tear that pussy up". "Barry you are hurting me, let me go". When I realized my demands were falling on deaf ears I kneed Barry right in the nut's. "Ahh what the fuck". Barry went down went a thud and I ran to grab my mace and phone. "Get the fuck out of here Barry before I mace your ass again. "Bitch this how you going to play me". "I'm calling the cops again this time they going to come lock your ass up. We are done lose my number ". With the threat of the police being called Barry limped out of my house and hopefully my life. As soon as Barry left I locked my doors and made sure my windows were secure and set my alarm. I didn't think he would be stupid enough to come back but better safe than sorry. After securing my house I called my mother and let her know what had taken place and checked in with Jerry. I also called my home girl Maxine and gave her the latest. "Girl you can't be serious he tried to rape you". Maxine was my best friend since middle school. She often tended to blow things out of proportion. " Girl he was just horny. If he wanted to rape me I don't think a little mase would have stopped him". Maxine sucked her teeth "you always act so nonchalant about shit like shit don't faze you. You know you was scared. You want me to come stay with you tonight?". I shook my head as if she could see me " I never said I wasn't scared I just don't see the point in blowing things out of proportion. What are you going to do with your bad ass kids if you come over here". "You mean your god sons I would bring them with me. We can have a little slumber party besides they are pretty much sleep anyway". "No I am fine I love my godson's but after the day and night I had I need to soak and get some rest I have to work in the morning". She sighed "ok call me tomorrow and let me know you're ok". With that I disconnected our call and soaked for about an hour after I made my way to bed for some much needed shut eye. Waking up the next morning my nerves were a little torn. I couldn't get Jerry out of my mind but I couldn't get Barry off my mind either. He stepped all the way out of line by showing up at my house unannounced. I had to get these men in check if I wanted to have a future with Jerry. Marshall was a whole other story I suspected he tried to lure me to the office for a hookup. I would deal with him as soon as I stepped in the office this morning. "Good morning Beautiful wanted to call and check on you I know we had an eventful day yesterday. Have to make sure you are able to get up and make it to work". There was that smile again "I am fine thank you for checking in on me. I'm heading out now I take it you're in the office already". Walking toward my car I noticed a trail of glass leading to my driver side window. "What the fuck". I ended up screaming into the phone after seeing my car window busted out it almost brought me to tears. I could not understand why my alarm didn't go off then I saw that it had been ripped out. "Jazelle are you ok" the sound of Jerry's voice brought me back to reality. "Yes Jerry i'm ok. I have to call you back". Without waiting I called the cops and my insurance company. The police arrived with an insurance agent in a rental and a tow truck. I told the police what transpired last night between Barry and myself and gave them everything I knew about him. I could not believe he would do something so juvenile like this. "Mam would you like to get a restraining order against Mr. Harris?". The officer asked me "yes". I had to be sure that this would never happen again. "You will have to come down to the station to complete the order". I had a hell of a morning " I will come in as soon as I get off of work". My phone would not stop ringing and looking who was headed my way I wish I would have answered. "Jerry I told you I was fine you did not need to leave work to come all the way over here". With the look of concern on his face Jerry runs to my side. "Yes I did, you sounded distraught". "We will see you down at the precinct this evening" the officer said handing me his card. Jerry began to look me over "are you ok, are you hurt". I sighed "i'm fine Jerry someone tried to break into my car that's all i'm ok". Jerry took one look at my car and lost it "who would do this to you. That's it i'm hiring you a bodyguard". I giggled a little and shook my head "That is not necessary Jerry The police will take care of this and I am not hurt". Jerry pulled me close to him "not another word I won't have the woman I love walk around here in harm's way". I was taken aback "the woman you what". Jerry quickly pulled me into a kiss and slightly weakened my defenses. "You heard me the woman I love. I know what I want Jazelle and that's you. It's ok if you're not ready to say it back I understand but I know how I feel and I am comfortable saying it". "Jerry I don't know what to say". "You don't have to say anything right now just know that I am going to do whatever it takes to protect you when I can't be around". I couldn't fight it anymore I was dick whipped which is why I ended up with a guard posted outside my office getting clearance for anyone who entered. I don't know what Jerry had that other men didn't but whatever it was made me want to change and be the best woman I could be for him. Walking into work that morning my mind was all over the place. I am normally cool as a fan but I would be lying if I said this morning's events had frazzled me. I gave Dean my new shadow pictures of everyone I would be willing to see today and strict instructions to send anyone else away. Busy at work time flew by and before I knew it lunch had approached and my stomach wouldn't let me skip. Packing up my things to head out I spotted Marshall approach my office door and Dean acting as a stop light preventing him from passing. "I am her co-worker I need to speak with her about a case". Marshall seemed very persistent. " Sorry sir you are not on the list of approved visitors so I will ask you to move along now". Dean was a man of his job but Marshall just had to pass "Jazzelle can you tell your bouncer to let me in, I need to go over this case with you". Against my better judgement I told Dean to let him in. "What can I do for you Marshall". He smiled and this time it had no effect on me whatsoever. "You have been avoiding me Jazzelle why is that". "I have been busy Marshall, why are you so eager to have me in your presence". He adjusted himself so I could see his print " we are co-workers for one. Two I was hoping we could have some more fun after all we both know I don't dissapoint". I shook my head "Marshall that was a one and done. I told you the day after we should have kept our parts to ourselves because we are co-workers. It was very clear we would not be making that mistake again. Now if you would excuse me I have plans". Walking out my office felt good normally there would have been this carnal urge to invite Marshall to lunch and enjoy some fun but I had no cravings for any other man meat but Jerry's. I didn't have as much time as I would have liked for lunch because I wanted to get ahead on some work so I could enjoy my weekend. I grabbed a sandwich from Panera Bread and sat outside to soak up some sun and fresh air before I headed back into the office. Checking my emails I felt like I was being watched. I kept taking discreet glances over my phone trying to make sure I didn't alert Dean. I slowly began to wrap my things up as the figure stalking me began to move quickly toward me. Before I could react Dean had the figure pinned down on the table. Struggling under Dean's grip Barry shouting profanity "You thought you could play me bitch". "Mam please go to the car I will take care of this degenerate". Without question I did as I was told on my way to the car I called my boss and told her I would not be back in which she cleared given what I had been through that morning she thought it was a good idea for me to be done with work for the day. After Dean spoke with the cops and they took Barry in I went to the police station to complete the restraining order. Jerry took very good care of me that evening. After taking care of everything at the police station and going home and packing my bags for the weekend Jerry insisted I come stay the night at his place and I did not resist. Jerry's home was immaculate with the hardwood floors , high ceilings, fireplace, shag rug, granite countertops, jacuzzi bathtub. You name it he had it. And he had plans for me that evening when I arrived he provided me with the warmest embrace. After the day I had it was welcomed. Scented candles and soul food met my nostrils. "There is a bath waiting for you. I just want you to relax and I will join you in a moment". "Ok" was all I could utter. In the bathroom more candles and a bath with rose petals and a chilled glass of red wine. The minute I soaked my body in the water it felt as if layers of my day began to melt away. Jerry came in shortly after completely naked with a waterproof massager in one hand and a tray of white chocolate covered strawberries in the other. I sat up to to take the tray from his hand but he pulled back "'no you sit back and relax,you have been through enough today". Jerry used one hand to massage me with the massager and fed me strawberries with the others. I didn't think I could relax anymore, that is until Jerry dried me off and massaged me with hot oil. Oh my god I was in heaven. He hit every nerve in my body. Every time I tried to return the favor I was dismissed. He wouldn't even let me feed myself. After a night of such relaxation I had no energy for much of anything not even sex. Jerry didn't seem to mind we just cuddled up in front of the fire and called it a night. I made sure I woke Jerry up that morning with some *rise and shine* action to show him how much I appreciated what he did for me last night. I made sure I used every jaw muscle imaginable and didn't let a drop of him go to waste. He tried to return the favor but for the first time I just wanted to make someone else feel good. "No that was for last night. Besides we have to get on the road we don't want to be late". The drive up to Jerry's parents house was a peaceful one we let the top down on his convertible and let the breeze soothe us. I took a nap and before I knew it we were parked in front of a beautiful summer two story home. It was breathtaking.

Jerry got out and opened my door "shall we". Taking his arm we walked to the door where Jerry walked in "I heard there were two old people who lived here but I don't see them". From behind the stairs a man's voice rang out "you need to clean your glasses boy cause I don't see any old folks here". Rounding the corner with a beautiful woman in her late fifties not far behind was a man who had to be Jerry's father besides the grey hair they could have been twins. The two men embraced "Hey pop". "Alright don't go hogging all the hugs save some for me". The woman swatted Jerry's father out of the way so she could get to her child and shower him with affection. "Now mama you know there will never be anyone who can take my hugs from you". As Jerry embraced his family I stood in awe at how much affection they showed one another. My mother and I were close but we did not gush over one another. "Mama, Daddy I have someone for you to meet. This is Jazelle.". I smiled and reached my hand out in an attempt to shake hands. "What is that thing girl we hug around here" and with that his mother pulled me into one of the warmest embraces I have ever felt. " I am Pearl you can call me mama pearl, Ms. P or just mama". "And i'm pops you can just call me pops". With that I met Jerry's parents with ease and it felt right. I thought it would be this uncomfortable weirdness this is why I think I avoided meeting any parents. "We are in the back son. The grill is fired up. Your brother is on his way, come on help me with these ribs. Jazelle I hope you eat meat because I make the best bar b que on the planet". I smiled slyly at Jerry "I love meat sir". Jerry gave me a wink letting me know he caught my reference."come on pop let's go before you burn up this food". Jerry had me so caught in a trance I nearly forgot where I was until mama Pearl snapped me back to reality. "Jazelle sweetie why don't come help me in the kitchen. I am finishing up the deviled eggs and mac and cheese". I smiled "I would love to help". "So Jazelle do you cook or are you more of a take out kind of girl". I laughed a little " I have been known to enjoy my fair share of pizza and chinese nights in but I know my way around a kitchen as well". She smiled "good answer I love my son but he has been known to keep company with the very pretty and pressed but not so domestic if you get my drift". Oh I got her drift this explained his assistance reaction when I came to his job. "You are very pretty I just want to make sure there's some substance, so what's your family like?". Trying to keep from sweating I took a deep breath "well my mother and I are close not as close as you guys are but we talk often. I have cousins but for the most part it's just us. My father didn't stick around long enough to actually be a father." She looked at me with so much sorrow in her eye's "no mama Pearl i'm fine my mother made a great life for me. I never wanted for anything I went to great schools and I have a great job. I am a well rounded human being as they say". I smiled hoping that would get her to lose some pity but that only got me a even sadder look and her coming around the island and giving me yet another hug. "So what can I help with?" . for the next thirty minutes we cut cheese sipped spiked lemonade and made potato salad and deviled eggs and laughed like old friends. By the time we got outside we were sharing inside jokes and giggling like school girls. "Well it looks like someone hit it off". Jerry came and wrapped his arms around my waist as I put the tray of food on the picnic table. "Well what's not to love". He nuzzled my neck "now which lady are you talking about because you know I love my mama, but you have my heart thumping and we all know you can do things my mama can't". "I would love to do those things to you right now especially the way you teasing my neck right now , but we are at your parents house. So I have to behave but when we get back and I mean as soon as we get back i'm going to do all those things your mama can't do". With that I turned around and planted a wet one on him and made a quick exit to the bathroom. I splashed some cold water on my face and wiped myself. Feeling Jerry push his thick stick up against me definitely had my kitty purring it took everything in me not to invite him in this bathroom and fuck his brains out, but that wouldn't go over to well with the parentals. After freshening up I made my way back to the backyard. I heard more chuckles and another voice added to the collective. When I came back outside Jerry reached for my hand "Jazelle this is my late brother Rico".

Carmon

Being a Virgin is not all it's cracked up to be, especially when you're a twenty five year old actress. Men tune in to desire you and assume you have all the experience in the world. Truth is I am surprised I made it this far without gifting my virtue to someone but truth be told my career has taken up a lot of my time and I have never been one to rush into anything. "Carmon you're needed on set in five". "Thanks Amber". On set of my hit show *Love in the stars* I am off to shoot another sex scene. Now for everyone on set this is just another walk in the park but for me and my hormones these scenes seem to get longer and harder everyday. My co star didn't help matters at all. Bryce Cooper was a six foot, toned, light skinned god. When we first started shooting I had a huge crush on him but after getting to know him the crush wore off but i'm still a hot blooded female. As I made my way to the set I got a glimpse of Bryce getting oiled up for our sex scene. I took a few deep breaths and assumed my position. "Action" after hours of shooting I couldn't wait to call it a night. Grabbing my things I couldn't wait to get home and soak away the day. "Hey Carmon great work today, see you tomorrow" Bryce stopped by my dressing room to say on his way out. "You too Bryce". In the car flashes of our scene danced in my mind. "Antonio all I ever wanted to do was love you". As Bryce looked into my eyes with such passion my panties began to moisten. " I know Claudette and i'm sorry for ever hurting you. I never wanted the smile to leave your face. I never wanted to be the reason why you stopped smiling". I turned my head slightly towards the camera to show off my forced tears. Bryce turned me to face him "Claudette I love you and I don't want to be with anyone else but you. I know how you are about words so let me show you". With that Bryce's lips met mine with such passion and my silky set wardrobe was now drenched with perspiration. Before I knew it my hand had found its way in my pants rubbing my swollen clit. "Antonio.." me as Claudette attempted to protest but to no avail. "Shh. Just let me show you how much I love you Claudette". Bryce began to plant soft kisses on my neck and my body reacted with so much pleasure. "Mmm Antonio" I moaned. Rubbing my clit even more I bit down on my lip to keep from alerting my driver of the joy I was giving myself. Bryce laid me on the bed and made a trail down my body. I felt myself about to reach my peak with the thought of Bryce's face between my legs. That's when I heard the divider began to roll down the partition. "Ms. Michaels we have arrived". "Thank you King". I composed myself before King, my driver could come around and open my door. I honestly don't know what has gotten into me, I never had a problem abstaining from sex before because I have never experienced it. Walking into my flat I began to shed my clothing and headed to the bathroom to run a well deserved bath. I grabbed my waterproof clit massager and soaked into the warm water while the bubbles washed over me I inhaled their fragrance. "Oh god Antonio I love you so much". I moaned as Bryce pretended to penetrate me. With every imaginary stroke I applied pressure to my swollen clit. Within minutes my body gave way as an explosion commenced beneath my waist. With my body fully relaxed I soaked for an hour and went to bed. I would love to say that sleep was peaceful but another wet dream rocked my body throughout the night. Tossing and turning with a faceless lover I woke up the next morning sweaty and horny yet again. After a cold shower I knew I had to get things back on track so a workout would shake the nerves. I ran to the park I was so zoned out I ran smack into what felt like a tree. After coming out of the dark I looked up to see the face of an angel hovering over me. "Miss are you ok?". After all the little birdies stopped flying around my head I was able to respond "yes thank you". After the angel helped me off the ground I took in all of him. Standing at what looked to be 5'9 , body built and the creamiest dark chocolate skin I ever seen on this planet. "Are you sure you're ok miss..". I realized I may have been drooling a little I shook my head from side to side. "Ms. Michaels, yes I am ok Mr..". He smiled revealing the most amazing set of teeth "Carter, Carter Finnx". Reaching out his hand to shake mine I realized I was staring again. "Nice to meet you". "I feel as if we've met before. Do you run here often". I smiled a little "no not that often and I think I would remember meeting you". As if just realizing he was still shaking my hand he stopped mid shake "are you sure you don't need me to take you to the hospital or walk you to your car". "I'm ok I ran here". "Oh ok would you at least let me walk you home to make sure you're safe and don't fall out on your way". I shook my head yes because I was afraid if I said anything my true feelings would come out of my mouth. About three blocks in Carter broke the silence "so have you lived around here for long?". "No I moved here about a year and a half ago for work","Oh ok what kind of work do you do?, if you don't mind me asking". "No I don't mind, i'm an actress" I spit it out quickly because I normally don't have a chance to say it people normally recognize me. I must say it was refreshing just to walk and conversate with someone and them not ask me a million questions about being on set and the work i've done. "Wow I never met an actress before what would I know you from". I thought about the commercial I shot when I was eighteen which was nationwide "I was in a pretty popular Fancy Girl deodorant commercial when I was younger now I am one of the stars of *Love in the stars*". His eyes lit up with recollection "I did see that commercial a while back you were the girl on the horse who looked nervous at first then you used the deodorant you rode with such poise and grace". I couldn't help but blush.

"You remembered the entire commercial". Now it was his turn to blush "well in my defense we play it at my job often". "Oh , where do you work if you don't mind me asking". He shook his head no "I am a flight attendant". "Really I haven't walked and talked with a flight attendant before". Carter burst into laughter "well I am glad I could be your first". That statement sent a jolt through my body and alerting my clit why I went running in the first place. Carter must have sensed the change because he changed the subject "I can't believe you ran this far we are about fifteen blocks in and haven't stopped. Are we close to your place?". Looking around I realized I have ran a ways away from my flat. "Umm, we have about seven more blocks to go. You don't have to walk the rest of the way if i'm taking you out your way". "No, I said I would make sure you got home safe and I mean that". For the rest of the walk we talked about favorites and work. Once we arrived at the corner of my block I decided I deserved a smoothie. "Would you like a smoothie?, my treat". "Sure why not I don't have any plans today". I smiled so hard. "Great my favorite place is right here, they make the best smoothies". Walking in I could tell the shop just opened which was perfect that gave me an opportunity to enjoy my smoothie without being mobbed by fans. "Cici, sweet Carmon how are you". I smiled at Mika the owner who always took care of me. His thick spanish accent made it hard to understand him sometime but he was adorable. "Mika this is Carter, Carter Mika. Mika is a smoothie god". Mika blushed "oh Cici how you make me blush, you big star love you make me blush in front of you friend".we all giggled "so what are you in the mood for" I rubbed my chin pretending to think "hmm I would like a sweet , energized kick with a relaxing undertone."I winked at the last of my request because Mika knew I meant my hormones. He winked back "and for the gentleman, what would you like?". Carter's eyes darted from myself to Mika with confusion on his face. Mika and I burst into laughter "Carter how it works is you tell Mika what mood you're going for and he makes a smoothie based on the mood you would like". "Oh ok Feel me makes sense now. It's also a good name for a massage parlor". Mika smiled from ear to ear "you see my vision. I am adding a spa expansion in the back. It will be how do you say very therapeutic". "Wow great minds right, well ok let me have some energy with a smooth cool aftertaste". Mika grinned more " ok you two have a seat and

I will bring your smoothie right over". After about five minutes Mika brought over our drinks. " For you senior smooth and cool. For you my lady sweet and relaxing". "Thank you Mika, ok Carter take a sip and let us know what you think". Being a bit dramatic he sniffed it "smells vibrant, looks like it has lots of body". With that he looked over at me causing me to blush and moisten. After taking a sip his eyes lit up "this is delicious Mika what did you put in this". Mike beamed with pride "I can't tell you that senior but if you keep coming back I promise you'll never be disappointed". With that Mika disappeared into the back of the shop. 'I'm glad you like it, although I had no doubt". He smiled "right smoothie god" we laughed "so you come here often?". "When I can yes. Mika was one of the first people to welcome me to the city when I moved here. I love his energy. I also love the fact that he respects my privacy". "It sounds like you have a good friendship. Is it safe to say it's just a friendship". His question caught me off guard "Yes, I mean he's been great to me. He delivers smoothies to me when it's packed and we talked about everything including playing for the same team amongst other things that kept us in the friend zone". After taking in what I said Carter let out a sigh of relief "that's great I wouldn't want to step on any toe's when I ask you to dinner tonight". My eyes lit up "oh wow,umm. Ok sure". Before I knew it I was at home getting ready for a date with a stranger that I literally ran into. It all reminded me of a movie. I found myself thinking of all the happy endings we could have. My thoughts were interrupted by my phone ringing. It was my agent Tina. "Hello Tina what do I owe the pleasure of this call so late in the evening". Tina giggled "Carmon honey it only 7:30 you should be out enjoying the nightlife, but not to much we don't need any PR nightmares". I smiled thinking about Carter "I actually have a date tonight". "Oh that's wonderful, is he on the team or is he into sports or a prince. What kind of publicity are we looking at". I shook my head "Tina this is my personal life not for the world. So can we please get to the reason why you are calling me after business hours". "Honey you are a celebrity there is no such thing as personal life, but i'll leave it alone for now. I'm calling because a box office movie just came across my desk with the most amazing role and deal for you. I need to see you first thing tomorrow morning so we can go over the details. So make sure you don't have too much of a good time tonight". "Ok Tina I will see you in the morning thanks for the call". "Make sure you get some good photos this evening, publicity is always great". I sighed "good night Tina". I spent the next 20 minutes applying makeup and narrowing down an outfit. I finally settled on a purple backless Omar Mansoor dress with slits in the side. My silver Roger Vivier stilettos really set the outfit off. I found myself excited, it had been awhile since i'd been on a date, I stopped trying after my last fiasco with Don Jerome. We were set up by our agents after shooting Global Guidance. The movie was great and on the set he was perfect. He was a complete gentleman. After about two dates I told him that I was a virgin and had no plans on putting out. Well all the gentlemen left the building and his agent called my agent to terminate the relationship. Talk about mortified, he didn't even have the common decency to break up with me himself. I saw him at one of my Premiere of Home to the heart and he had the nerve to say we could pick it up where we left off. What a joke. Deciding to wear my hair up or down my intercom buzzed. Looking at the camera I could see Carter looking very dapper in his Tasso Elba suit from his latest collection. I grabbed my clutch purse and made my way down. "Wow , you look beautiful". I blushed "thank you, you look nice as well". He smiled "I try, thank you". After our pleasantries Carter led me to his car a 2017 BMW 230i. "Nice car for a flight attendant". "It' an investment besides I do more than be a flight attendant". Curiosity peaked I asked "so what else do you do?". "I have my own car wash, it brings in a pretty good profit". I love a man with ambition "so what made you become a flight attendant?". He smiled "I love to travel so once my business was stable I hit the skies". I smiled back "wow you have so many layers to you". "Oh this is my song" and with that Carter turned the radio up and blaring from the speakers was Jesse Powell "You". As Carter sang along I could hear he had a pretty good voice something else to add to the pros list. We decided to head to Marjolin's an upscale french restaurant that I loved and I happen to know the owner who always had a table in the back for me. "Can you pull around back please". Carter did as I requested and we ended up in the kitchen of the restaurant. "Bella" I turned to see the owner Boyce smiling at me. "Hey Boyce" giving him a hug I could since the need for explanation. "Boyce this is Carter , Carter this is Boyce". "Bonjour monsieur" they shook hands. "Right this way Bella I have your table set up for you and your guest". As we sat the waiter came out with a bottle of 2007 Domaine Josmeyer Alsace "Bella for your table. I will send Marcel right out to take your order". "Thank you Boyce". Carter smiled at me "another one of your gods i'm guessing". I giggled "Their food is great and Boyce looks out for me as well. This is one of the few restaurants I can go to without making an appearance. Boyce lets me come in as well and enjoy my food. His wife makes sure of it." I laughed and Carter laughed with me. I watched Carter eyeball the menu for a moment . "Bonsoir je peux prendre votre commande?" Marcel came to the table and asked. Carter looked confused for a moment. I giggled, "how may I take your order monsieur?" . "Carter would you mind if I ordered for the table?". "Be my guest". His smile gave me chills "Il va falloir, deux Nicoise salad and Confit de canard Pour moi et pour le Monsieur Beef bourguignon". " tout de suite Miss" and with that Marcel went to put in our order. Carter smiled at me "I am in awe right now, did you just order food". I laughed "yes you are going to love it, it is a meat and potatoes kind of dish. I have to keep my languages down for work". "Well i'm impressed my last date could barely speak english let alone any other language". We laughed "i'm just glad you didn't feel emasculated with me ordering for you". "I am a real man I don't get hung up on things like that"."Note taken". We talked and Carter continued to win points. Our food got to us and I was reminded how hungry I really was. "Wow this looks amazing, i'm glad you didn't order me any snails". We laughed and drank another bottle of wine. By the end of dinner I felt as if I had known Carter my entire life. Marcel returned to the table to take our dessert orders "what are some specials tonight". "Certainly Ms. This evening we have our creamy Crème brûlée, our yummy Crêpes and our silky smooth Far Breton". "Carter would you like order dessert for us?". "Sure, we will take one of everything". We laughed. "So tell me something why is a beautiful, smart, successful woman like yourself single". I pondered the question for a moment. "I am very selective in who I let in my life. In my experience you can't always trust everyone. I also work a lot and most men don't find it attractive when I have to travel to another state or out of the country to kiss other men". He chuckled "sounds like you have been dealing with some insecure men. Men who are secure in themselves don't mind their woman going out making a living for herself. It's a good thing you ran into me". We laughed. Heading home I felt myself getting anxious. I knew I wanted to kiss him. Well way more than kiss him but that would break all my rules. I don't kiss on the first date and I have never given it up. So the walk to the door had my nerves going. "I hope you enjoyed yourself tonight". A nervous smile spread across my face. "I had a blast I haven't laughed so much in my life". With every step my palm became even wetter than my panties. "I'm glad. I've never been out with a superstar don't want to end up in one of those tabloids as the worst date you ever had". I laughed "I wouldn't discuss my personal business with any outlets and I most certainly wouldn't lie". His smile disarmed me and before I knew it our lips had met and we entered into an intense tongue battle. After taking a breath I pulled back and reached for the door handle. "Thank you Carter for the lovely evening. Talk to you soon". I ducked into my flat and ran for my vibrator. I quickly released myself from my clothes and went to town on my clit. After giving myself the release I desperately needed I took and nice long shower and called it a night. The next morning I headed to Tina's office to read this blockbuster she claimed to have for me. Heading into the office I received a text from Carter ~*Good Morning Beautiful I hope your morning is going well. I would love to take you out tonight. Let me know*~ . I couldn't stop smiling. "There's my favorite client, with a smile on her face. Someone scored last night". "Good morning to you too Trina". "Darling it's a great morning. Your next project is going to make us both able to retire". I looked at her as if she was crazy "Retire, let me see this script because it must be made of gold if you are talking like a true crazy person". Looking at the title I couldn't get a feel for what the movie was about. *"But I didn't say no* what is this about?" . Trina gave me the biggest smile "it's about this girl who thinks she got raped but is not sure. This movie will show your range and get you so many other opportunities". "Rape, really this is a deep topic. I'm a good actress but I have never been in that situation I don't know if I can pull that off". "Listen go home and and read the script, get a feel for it. This role is just what you need to get you out of the romance box". "Fine Trina. Is this all you have for me?". "You have a press packet for the new season of *Love in the stars.* Here's your schedule tonight you have the *Daily late show* so if I were you I would head home and rest up for the night". "Trina I wish you would give me more advanced when it comes to these things. How do you know I didn't have plans this evening". "That's the beauty of a raincheck honey. Now go read and rest and call me in the morning with the good news". Leaving Trina's office I felt a little pissed that she just drops these things in my lap at the last minute. Looking at the schedule I saw that I had promos set up for the rest of the week so I knew I needed to head over to Nina my stylist to get me a few looks. Once I got to Nina's I text Carter back with the bad news ~*Hey handsome I had a great time too. I really want to hang out again soon but I have to work tonight. For the rest of the week actually, but I will make time for us to hang out after my press junket xoxo~*. "Hey Carmon how are you". Nina greeted me with a warm smile. "Hey Nina i'm good. I just need a few looks for press this week". "Did you bring your schedule?". I handed over my schedule and followed her to the fitting room. "It would be nice if Trina would go digital and save us both the last minute hassle". I laughed "you and me both". For the next hour Nina and I went over so many different looks until we finally settled on six looks for me. "Thank you Nina". She smiled "no problem, I will have them delivered to you this evening". Pulling up to my flat I noticed a figure standing out front. I started to go around back then I realized I knew the figure. There stood Carter with a picnic basket in hand. "Well isn't this a pleasant surprise. What are you doing here?". That million dollar smile graced his face. "I wanted to surprise you. After you told me how busy your schedule was I thought you could use a nice meal before your busy week started". I smiled so hard I could feel my cheeks began to hurt. "That is so sweet thank you". I lead Carter into my flat and he set up a picnic area for us next to my fireplace. "So what is on the menu tonight chef" I asked with a hint of a giggle in my throat. "Well it's no boofbeno or whatever it was you ordered for me but it's eatable". I laughed "well what do we have". Carter pulled out two gourmet salads, two alfredo pastas with grilled chicken breast and two smoothies from Mika's. "Wow you went all out. Hat's off to the chef". We ate and talked and before I knew it we were making out heavy. We were rubbing and touching, getting really steamy. After I thought I would burst my bell rang. Saved by the bell you could say. Nina sent over the looks for my hectic week. "Clothes delivered, most people just go shopping". "Haha I am like most people, I shopped earlier and after some altering my stylist sent over what I picked out". "Ahh I see so not a total diva that's good". I didn't know how to take that so I thought it would be best to end the night here. "Well I have had a lovely evening. Thank you for doing this but now I need to get ready for my crazy week ahead". He gave me an awkward smile "Oh ok. I did too , I hope I didn't offend you". "Oh no, I know it was a joke I just have a lot to do for work that's all". "Ok let me clean all this up and I will get out of your hair so you can get to work". "Oh no I can clean this up if you don't mind me returning your basket and tupperware at a later date". "Ok fine" he leaned in and gave me a kiss on the cheek. "I'll call you later". With that Carter left and I prepared to get to work. After cleaning up I ran a long bubble bath and grabbed the script and a bottle of wine. Sinking into the tub and the script after about two hours I felt totally relaxed and in love with this script. I called Trina to let her know I was in. Picking up my phone I saw a text from Carter ~*hey I hope you are not upset with me*~. I called Trina before I texted back. "Trina i'm in". She cheered on the other end of the phone "Great choice darling. You're wanted in New York in exactly one month I will send you the details". I was lost "New York, I thought we would be filming here because of the show. "No Carmon you will film your next twenty episodes this month and then off to New York you go"."Trina I need to think about this. I just got settled and I love the show. What would they do about my storyline and I have a contract what will happen to that. I just don't know Trina". "Carmon honey listen you will fulfill your contractual duties and I will speak with them about your role moving forward. As far as moving you are an actor honey it comes with the job. I will let you sleep on it but we have to get on this before they start looking at their other choices". With that Trina hung up the phone and left me with my thoughts. I rubbed my body down with my therapeutic oils and laid down for a well deserved nap. Before I knew it my alarm was alerting me that my car would be downstairs in thirty minutes. I decided on a money green spaghetti strap dress with enough sparkles to blind *Stevie Wonder* . I received another text from Carter while I napped. ~*I guess so*~. I decided to put him out of his misery. ~*No I am not upset with you. True I didn't like your brand of humor but i'm not upset. But we should do lunch soon I would like to talk to you about something. Have a good night*~. In the studio I was escorted the green room where I watched the show until it was time for me to go on stage. *Kevin Hart* was out on stage tearing up everyone's sides.

"Carmon you are up after this break". "Thank you". After the host Brandon Staples introduced me I made my way on the stage with a wave and a smile. After about five minutes of witty banter between the three of us Bradon got down to business. "So Carmon I love the show, you get very hot and steamy. Is there anyone keeping it hot and steamy in your life right now". Not surprised by the question I gave him the same response I give everyone. "I am focused on my career right now". After figuring out he wasn't going to get me to dish on my love life he moved on and focused on my career and Kevin's life. All in all the show was great. After the show I headed home for a much needed rest. Sitting in front of my door was a dozen roses with a note~*I apologize for my lame humor. I look forward to seeing you soon xoxo Carter*~ . I went to sleep with a goofy grin on my face. The next morning I text Carter thanking him for my flowers and inviting him to lunch so we could talk. After a long day of shooting it was time for a break. We were given a five hour break in between shooting because our director had a meeting to get to regarding the direction of the show. For the life of me I couldn't understand why he couldn't schedule the meeting when we weren't shooting or get someone else to direct but I wasn't complaining. This gave me more time to spend with Carter. After getting in my normal clothes I met Carter a few blocks away at a little bistro. After signing some autographs I found Carter sitting in the back in a booth. "Hey i'm so happy to see you". "Me too" I smiled as he stood and kissed my cheek. "Thank you for my roses again". He smiled at me "I was really sorry about my joke gone wrong, and I definitely didn't want to lose what we just started". "Yeah about that..". "Good afternoon may I take your order". The waiter cut me off before I could finish my thought. "I will have the Arugula Salad and a lemonade" I quickly ordered hoping to get back to my conversation. "You sir". Carter took his time looking over the meu. "Everything looks so good, do you have any suggestions". I didn't know if he was talking to me or the waiter but I took the opportunity to get this show on the road. "He will have the Lamb duo hold the onions and a pineapple juice". The waiter looked to Carter for confirmation before he went to put the order in. After he nodded the waiter took our menus "I will be right out with your meal". Carter took my hand "if I knew you wanted to order for me I wouldn't have looked at the menu". I let out a nervous giggle. "I mean i'm kind of an expert at it now". He laughed "you are 1-0 so far". I took a deep breath "i'm moving to New York". I blurted out the words hoping it would lift some weight off my shoulders. It did not. I looked up at Carter who was staring back at e with a confused look on his face. "What?". I explained the movie deal to him and how everything would start in a month. He sat and listened before responding. Before I knew it our waiter had come back to the table with our meals. "Enjoy". Carter looked down at his plate "this looks great. I think you might be 2-0". I smiled waiting for him to address what I said. "Congratulations on the movie Carmon that's big". With that he dug into his food leaving me lost on where to go with the conversation. I wanted to ask what about us, I wanted to know if we were done after this lunch. Wanted to know if he would be open to a long distance relationship work. Why hadn't he said anything about us dating or fighting for me. I knew it was early but I expected something. I thought we were closer. I guess not. "Mmm this is delicious. Carmon strikes again". I smiled. "Why aren't you eating did you change your mind about what you wanted". I looked down at my untouched salad "oh no it's fine. I honestly expected the conversation to go another way". He looked confused "What did you expect Carmon?". "I expected for us to talk about us moving forward. If there would be an opportunity of us continuing what we started". I felt as if I was pouring my heart out and I was alone in my feelings. After a long pause he finally broke the silence. "Carmon I never planned on ending what we started and I didn't want to give you the impression that I was having second thoughts because of your movie. I wanted you to feel good about your movie this is big I will be here for you every step of the way". I couldn't stop the smile from spreading across my face. "Well ok that makes me feel a lot better". I ate and got back to the set. After shooting all day I had a few press runs that evening. I made it home around 2am. After getting about three hours of sleep I headed to the radio station to do some interviews. After I stopped at three radio stations two morning shows and had four phone interviews it was time to head back to the set. "Carmon honey you look wiped out let's get you to the refreshing chair quickly. We start shooting in 15". The Director bombarded me before I could get on the lot good. I didn't even address him I just went to my dressing room to put down my bags. "Hi Carmon can I get you anything" my assistant Tibby addressed me when I walked in. "Hi Tibby, yes can you please get me a fruit salad and let Lisa know I need a refresher before hair and make-up". Tibby fluttered off to complete my request. I changed into my wardrobe and sat in my chair while Lisa applied my refreshing mask. While the mask set I ate my fruit salad and got my hair done. I loved my team on the set everyone was so efficient. I never had a late day to set and today was no different. I stood on my mark ready to deliver an award winning performance but it seems as if my co-stars didn't get the memo. "Where the hell is Jessica and Robin" the director yelled out looking at me as if I had them in my back pocket. Robin's assistant handed the director a phone. "Why the hell aren't you here. What? . This is unacceptable I will have your jobs do you hear me hello...hello.". After receiving no response the director smashed the phone down. "Shooting is canceled for today. I will contact you later on with the new shooting schedule". Others huffed I just went to my dressing room to get changed. "Carmon do you need anything else before you go". "No Tibby. Thank you". "Thank you Carmon, because of you I have a stable job". I looked at Tibby lost and confused. "Out of all the actors on set you are the most professional and you never degrade me. With Robin and Jessica getting fired their assistance lose a job too". I never thought of it like that. All I ever did was try to make sure I did my job and did it well. "Tibby I appreciate the work you do and i'm sorry for your friend's. Maybe they'll get to be the replacements assistance". Tibby shook her head "no, one of them is Robin's cousin she only hired her because she likes to get high and she didn't want anyone from the outside to know about it, but she treats her cousin so bad that she gossips with the rest of us about everything that goes on". My mind went over everything I did on set and wondered if there was any gossip going around about me. As if Tibby was reading my mind she responded to my thoughts "we never talk about you Carmon everyone on the set loves you". I let out a slight sigh of relief "Well i'll see you tomorrow Tibby". With that I left the building. I called Carter and told him to meet me at the spa. After the few days I had I needed to be pampered and I wanted to see how rugged Carter really was. Pulling up to the spa I spotted Carter standing outside with flip flops on and a big grin on his face."Hey beautiful. You ready to be pampered because I am". He leaned in and planted a wet one on me. "It's well deserved". We took our places in the chairs for our mani pedis and let the pampering commence. After about three hours of massages, masks and wraps we were so relaxed I felt as if I were floating on a cloud. "So now what Ms. Carmon". I mulled it over for a moment "we can go to your place". He looked shocked but recovered smoothly "ok sounds great". I followed Carter to his house I have to say I was impressed. He had a beautiful tudor home it looked like it was made for a family. Carter came and opened my door and we walked hand and hand to his front porch. Walking inside I was surprised to see kids toys in the living room. Looking to Carter for an answer I found myself getting nervous waiting for the response. "I am a big brother to a rambunctious six year old and sometimes I bring him here to play or bring his friends and hosts sleepovers. I would've told you if I had a child. The big brother program is important to me I would like for you to meet Anthony one day he's a great kid". I let out the breath I was holding in "I would love to". Carter just seemed to get better and better. "Make yourself at home. Are you hungry we can order some food". "I could eat ". We spent a lovely afternoon together enjoying indian food, wine , Netflix shows and great conversation. By the time night was upon us we had found ourselves hold up with no expectations of leaving. I was having so much fun I forgot all about work and the stress of life. Trina brought me back to reality real quick. "Carmon you have a premier in an hour. Your hair and makeup team is at your house why aren't you there". Carter and I were having such a good time I completely blanked on the premier but I couldn't tell Trina that. "Oh my god Trina I completely forgot about the premier I got so pampered at the spa I feel asleep. I have been going non-stop and it's not even my premier I could stand to miss this one Trina". She let out a loud scoff "Carmon this is a premier for the stars, it's a who's who for who's who. You should be there to show your face and get ready for your big movie. This is the set up for your run. This is how the business works. You can't miss a night because that could be the night a music producer shows up and wants you in the next Chris Brown video. Or you could meet Denzel Washington and he thinks you have raw talent. These are the things you go through to keep your star shining bright. Now I am sending over the key to let the team in I expect you to be there to prepare for this premiere. Toodles". With that Trina hung up giving me no room for response. "You have to go". I looked at Carter with an apology in my eyes. "Yes , but I don't want to". Just then a lightbulb went off in my head. "Would you like to come with me?". Carters eyes widened with shock and to be honest I shocked myself. "Are you comfortable with that". I thought about it for a second. "Yes, I mean it's a premier and it's not my movie. We wouldn't walk the carpet together. It's a dark theater no one would know we know each other. I can get Trina to get you a ticket. Do you have a suit". He nodded his head yes. Before I knew it I was back on the phone with Trina getting her to score me an extra ticket. After evading a million questions she finally got it done. After forty five minutes we were dressed and ready to head out. "You look beautiful". I blushed "you look very handsome". The entire ride to the premier Carter and I made out like two teenagers. Before stepping out of the car I touched up my makeup and made sure my dress was wrinkle free. Stepping out of the car my black and silver sparkling ballroom gown caught the flashing lights of the cameras as I walked the carpet. As I stood on the carpet and listened to the normal chants "Who are you wearing, what's next for you, turn this way". My mind was dead set on the fact that I would see Carter inside. I felt like a young girl about to see my crush. I smiled and posed for a few pictures before I made my way to the side for a few interviews. I couldn't wait to get inside. After grabbing a few gourmet snacks I made my way inside the theater and headed in Carter's direction but before I could get to him Don Jerome stepped into my path. "My sweet Carmon I knew you would come back to me". Confusing written all over my face I looked at him for an answer to clear things up for me. "Trina called and told me how you wanted a ticket for me to join you so i'm here to save the day honey". I tried my best to keep my rage inside. "Don I apologize for Trina's mistake trust me she will be dealt with. I did not ask for another ticket for you in fact my guest is here and seated. So if you would excuse me I am going to enjoy the movie. Have a good night". With that I made my way to my seat to join Carter and I made a mental note to call Trina and give her a piece of my mind. "I started to get nervous I thought you ditched me". I smiled at Carter "why would I ditch the most handsome man here".The movie was great at least the parts I saw. Truth is Carter and I spent most of the movie playing footsie and in a heated tongue battle. Before the credits Carter and I agreed to mingle for a few minutes then he would head to the car. I stopped in the ladies room to check my makeup when I was cornered by Don's new ex fling Marisoul Flood. She was a reality star who was trying to make it big in the movie industry. From what I have seen she could stand to take some etiquette classes but that was not my place to say so. "I see you came to your senses and realized Don needed a real woman to please him. Thank you for letting go I was starting to get embarrassed for you". I took a deep breath and smiled politely "that's funny because I have always been embarrassed for you. Don came here to be my date and then when I turned him down he went to find you. Looks to me like you should save that pity for yourself. Now if you would excuse me I need to go congratulate my peers on a job well done. I'm sure there's a reunion for you to go fight at. Have a good night". With that I left her standing there with her mouth gaped open. Such a sad little girl but again not my problem. I went to praise the cast and mingle with a few industry friends. I saw Don and Marisoul having a heated discussion that got very loud before they were asked to leave. I just shook my head had a drink and called my driver. Standing by the bar waiting to hear my driver had pulled out front I saw my co star Bryce. "Hey Bryce, how are you". He came and hugged me which his date did not seem to happy about. "Hi Carmon I am good". He looked me up and down "You look amazing". I smiled politely "you look nice as well and so does your date. I love your dress". I focused on his date trying to ease some of the tension. That seemed to work because she smiled and shook my hand eagerly. "Thank you Carmon, I love your dress too. My name is Brittany". I smiled "nice to meet you Brittany and thank you". Bryce looked frustrated to say the least. I had seen this look before. Bryce was unhappy with the fact that he was at yet another event with a woman he had no interest in dating. He like myself wanted to keep his dating life very private so I knew his fiance slash best friend and bodyguard Jerod was close by. Bryce and I had become close over the past year we spent on set and we even hung out every once and awhile. One night we got very drunk and Bryce kissed me. I was nervous but excited. I had a crush on him so it was kind of a dream come true but for Bryce it just confirmed what he already knew. He broke down and cried and told me everything that night. I told him about my virginity and ever since it has been like an unspoken bond between us. "I wish I would have known you were here we could have sat together" Bryce said. Thinking back to my steamy tryst with Carter in the theater I was glad we didn't but I wouldn't tell him that. "Yeah me too". My phone went off alerting me my driver was out front. "Are you going to the after party Carmon" Brittany asked me. "No I have an early morning tomorrow. It was nice meeting you". With that I headed to the car. With a smile on his face Carter greeted me with a wet warm kiss that made my insides ignite with heat. Carter broke our kiss "go away with me". At that moment I would have agreed to anything "when?". "Right now. I don't have a private jet but I can get us first class flights with private cabin". Before I could think I was giving the driver instructions to take me home to pack a bag and stop by Carter's place. Before I knew it We were in our private cabin snuggled up and kissing. Trina objected saying I had more press to do. I kindly reminded her that her assumptions this evening could have caused a huge scene. With that she quickly cleared my schedule with no more protest. "Where are we headed , I know we are going to Detroit but what part, are we getting a hotel". I had so many questions. Although I was a star I never rarely did things this spontaneous. I have to schedule free time so this was a new thing for me."You will see when we get there. I promise you will love it just relax". That's exactly what I did for the rest of the flight. Carter and I made our way to a cabin which was very secluded. I loved the idea that we would have some more alone time together. "Took y'all long enough. Well come on I already got the fire started". A brown skinned woman with bright brown eyes stepped onto the porch startling me, so much for alone time. Carter took my hand and led me inside. "Mom this is Carmon , Carmon this is my mother Liza". I shook her hand nervously "Nice to meet you " I said trying to hide the surprise in my voice. "Same here with everything Chucky has told me I feel like I already know you". I looked over at Carter for clarity. "Chucky is mamas nickname for me". I giggled a little. "Chucky don't just stand there show Carmon to your room so y'all can get washed up for dinner". Without a second thought Carter grabbed my hand and rushed me up the stairs to a room at the end of the hall. Before I could sit down Carter pulled me into his arms and planted a passionate kiss on my lips. After catching my breath I asked "what was that for". He smiled "you are so genuine and pure. I am happy I brought you to meet my mom". I blushed "we better hurry up and get washed up for dinner". I gave Carter a peck on the lips and made my way to the bathroom in the room. When I came out I headed back down the stairs to join Carter and his mother. "Do you need help with anything?". Liza smiled at me "you know how to make lemonade sugar?". I gave her big bright smile "yes mam ". I followed Liza into the kitchen where a half filled pitcher sat on the counter and lemons spread across the counter."Knock yourself out. I'm going to get cleaned up for dinner". I took a deep breath and dived in. after about two minutes of struggling with the juicer Carter came to rescue me. "This is a test. My mom wants to see if you can rough it". He took the juicer from my hand and pulled out an electric juicer from the cabinet. "This is how she does now here let's give you a fighting chance". I smiled at Carter with great appreciation in my eyes. Within minutes the lemons were squeezed and I made my special mix and garnished it with a touch of mint. I poured Carter a little in a cup so he could taste it. "Mmm sweet, but not as sweet as you. Come here". With that Carter lifted me into his arms planting wet kisses on my lips and face. I giggled " enough of all that horse playing in my kitchen". Liza's voice brought our play to an abrupt halt. "Come on bring the food out so we can eat". Without hesitation but with a little giggle we brought the food to the table. Looking at the fried chicken, mashed potatoes, corn on the cob, biscuits and collard green I knew I would have to skip breakfast and run an extra mile tomorrow. My mouth salivate just looking at it and smelling the lovely aroma. "Carmon would you like to say grace" Liza asked snapping me out of my trance. "Sure" with that we joined hands while I led us in blessing the food and thanking Liza for welcoming into her home. When I looked up Liza seemed impressed and Carter had a proud smile on his face. "Well let's dig in before it gets cold". We ate and talked, Liza didn't grill me as bad as I thought she would. My stomach was so full but the food was so good could not stop eating. "I love a girl with a healthy appetite but save room for dessert" Liza said to me noticing I was putting it away. I smiled bashfully. Liza left the table and returned with a triple layer walnut chocolate cake. I had to wipe up the drool that slid from my mouth. Before I could protest Liza sat a slice in front of me and began to drizzle caramel sauce on it. Forget skipping breakfast I would have to skip both breakfast and lunch. The first bite blew my mind. After devouring my cake Liza asked me to come to the living room where she showed me pictures of Carter while he cleaned the dishes. We laughed at all the adorable pictures of Carter. Carter joined us in the living room shortly after. "Why do I feel like i'm being talked about". I smiled at Carter "because i'm showing Carmon here all your business". Liza said with a giggle. After about an hour if chatting and looking at pictures Carter and I retired to our room. I attempted to gather my things for the shower but Carter had other plans. He pulled me onto the bed with him. "My mother feels the same way I feel about you". I looked at him feigning innocent "and how's that". He smiled and planted a soft kiss on my lips. "You love me" I asked loving the feeling but shocked at the same time. "To soon?" he asked. "No I was just surprised that's all. I love you too". With that Carter kissed me so passionately my soul felt it. We began to get hot and heavy. I contemplated on going all the way with Carter and if I should tell him I was a virgin. "Carter we have to stop". "Am I hurting you. Did I do something wrong?" he asked surprised by my abrupt pause. "No it's just that i'm a virgin". I couldn't read his face but he sat up abruptly as if the bed were on fire. "Are we talking born again virgin or virgin virgin" . "Vigin vgirgin. I am a virgin meaning I have never been with a man in that way". Carter looked at me as if I had two heads. "Would you like me to sleep in another room". I was a bit disappointed by his reaction but I wasn't surprised. He must have seen the disappointment in my face "no i'm sorry I just want you be comfortable". "Carter we have been in each others personal space why would me being a virgin suddenly change that now". I felt the tears began to well up in my eyes so I grabbed my things and ran into the bathroom before a tear could fall. I heard Carter knock on the door a few times but I ignored him. I climbed into the shower and the hot water drown my sorrows. When I entered the room Carter was nowhere in sight but a letter was on the bed. *"I am sorry Carmon, I would never do anything to intentionally hurt you. I have never been in this situation. Everything is new to me from your status to you being a virgin. I apologize if I hurt you that is the last thing I ever wanted to do. I meant what I said I love you and if you would allow me I would love to cuddle with XOXO Carter"*. I cried a little but this time it was happy tears. I rushed out to find Carter and ran smack into him just like the first time we met. This time he caught me and held me in his arms. "I'm so sorry baby". That night Carter held me and made me feel so safe. *Six month later.* Carter had given me everything I could ask for in a man and a relationship. He had been patient with me filming and waiting until I was comfortable with us going public. Tonight was the night I planned a big birthday bash for Carter and I invited a few of my celebrity friends and close friends from the press. Trina was so elated she offered to pay for everything. I told her she should save her money for a great gift. The movie did so well I didn't have to work for awhile so I planned to go away with Carter so we could enjoy each other. My show had wrapped for the season so I had plenty of time. My character had been in a coma while I shot the movie and escaped from the hospital with amnesia while I did press. All in all I have a great team and they made sure I would be back next season. "Baby where are we going I told you I would've been happy if we stayed in and ordered food for my birthday" Carter complained as I guided him into the location of his surprise party. "I told you that is unacceptable. Besides you know I know the best places to get a great meal. Trust me". He sighed "I trust you Carmon". When we walked in everyone yelled surprise and Carter looked so shocked. I was so happy everything had gone according to plan. Liza came up to me and whispered in my ear "everything is set up" I nodded my acknowledgement. She hugged and kissed Carter and led us to the table where all of Carter's favorite were prepared. Carter's face lit up and he smiled at me and Liza. "You two are st full of surprises". With that he pulled us into a group hug. "I wish I could take the credit but this is all Carmon. She called me and set everything up". Carter gave me a passionate kiss. "Thank you". "You're welcome, isn't this better than takeout". He laughed "Way better". We danced a little and I introduced Carter to my friends that he hadn't yet met and he did the same. I even had a room set up for his little brother and friends. When we headed to our table we were stopped and asked to pose for pictures. Carter gave me a face that said are you cool with this. In response I planted a big wet one on his lips as the photographers snapped away. We posed for a few more then headed to our table where we feasted on all the good food Liza and my mother prepared. I was so glad our mothers got along and my mother loved Carter. The waiter came to clear our table Carter whispered something in his ear and he returned with a mic. Carter stood and the Dj to play the beat to "you" as Carter serenaded me. I melted in front of everyone then as the song was ending Carter got down on one knee and asked me to marry him. I almost fainted. Somehow I mustered the energy to say yes. Carter pulled me into his arm and kissed me. "Now who's full of surprises". Carter smiled "that's not all" I turned to see my stylist and Trina standing behind me with my mom. "What's going on". I asked a little confused. "You have to go get changed we have some marrying to do" Carter said. After about ten minutes of Carter explaining how he contacted Trina to set everything up but when I insisted we on going out he called to have Trina bring everything to his party which she already knew about. After a bit of hair and makeup and wardrobe change I headed towards the man of my dreams to become his wife. After we exchanged vows so many pictures were snapped it nearly blinded me. We headed the jet I had set up for our trip which would now be our honeymoon. When we arrived to the hotel there were a group of people waiting on us out front one had a sign that said welcome Mr and Mrs Finxx. I was shocked Carter really did have everything planned out. When we got to our room everything was set up beautifully rose petals on the bed, chocolate covered strawberries candlelight and carter's birthday cake that Liza made. A tear rolled down my face "are you ok baby" Carter asked with concern. I responded by giving him the most passionate kiss I could muster. With that Carter took the lead and removed my dress while leading me to the bed. When came out of his clothes the walls of virginia pulsated with anticipation. I laid before him in my birthday suite and I couldn't feel more loved and ready for what was about to take place. With every kiss on the trail to my virtue I became more aroused. When Carter's lips wrapped around my clit I lost it. My body jerked uncontrollably as I felt the mother of all explosions shoot out of me. Before I could compose myself Carter began to enter me. I was in so much bliss that I barely felt the pain when my cherry popped. I became even more wet and followed Cartes rhythm as we got into a groove I felt myself about to explode again. "I love you Carmon". "I love you too".

Damon

As I stroked to the sounds of *jodeci Freak you* it dawned on me that I didn't even remember this girls name. All I remember is she had a smile to die for, legs for days and it didn't take long to convince her to come back to my "smash pad" and dig her back out. Her tits were amazing, I nursed on them for about fifteen minutes when we first got into it. I think it was Erica or maybe Ashley. Time for the deep stoke game. "Oh my fucking gosh", gets them everytime. Her pussy is aight, I wish I could remember her name I would love to put her in rotation. Reaching for her shoulder so I could get deep in her guts I saw a tattoo where my thumb had been. *Dana and Mack 4life*. Dana that was her name, damn wasn't even close. Time for the grand finale. "Aww shit yeah take all this dick". Stroke , Stroke , smack. Repeat. "Fuck i'm about to nut". With that I pulled out and snatched off the condom and sprayed her back and ass with my seed. "Damn daddy your stroke game is mean. Where can I wash up". I pointed her in the direction of the bathroom in the corner of the room. While she cleaned herself up I called my homeboy to pick me up in five. His lame ass was still at the club trying to get some ass. When she came out the bathroom she made it known that she planned to stay awhile. I had other plans. "So you want to order some food?". I looked at her sideways "nah shorty i'm good. You should get dressed though our ride will be here any minute". By now I was fully dressed ready to head out. "Our ride. Oh so it's like that". Here comes the bullshit. "Look we had fun and I would love to do it again sometime. Our ride is going to take us back to the club so you can catch up with your girls". There it is the look of shock and disgust like she didn't just meet me and let me slide up in her. "We had fun. So you just going to play me and you expect me to want to fuck with you after this. Fuck you nigga". While she ranted and raved I texted Randy ~Code 7~. This was a code we created in high school that lets each other know the chick might get hostile hurry up. I just sat in silence while she hustled around the room to get dressed. Cussing me out the entire time. When she realized I wasn't responding she really got upset. "You just going to sit there with that stupid ass look on your face. You a foul ass nigga". I just looked at her for a moment before responding. "What makes me foul Dana, the fact that we met and after one drink you came up here with me to have sex. Or is it the fact that i'm not treating you like my girl. We are both grown, you knew what we were coming up here to do, I told you that in the club. I never disrespected you or lied to you. So can you please tell me what makes me foul Dana". "My name is Jessica, asshole". With that she stormed out of the apartment. "Then who the fuck is Dana" I called after her laughing. After waiting a minute I headed out myself and found Randy downstairs. "You had a lot of code 7's here lately. I think you're losing your touch" Randy said once I got in the car. I looked in the rearview mirror just in time to see Jessica get in a car full of females, as the car rode passed us Jessica flipped me the bird. I laughed "i'm just bored. These chicks make it to easy". Randy laughed "you trying to go back to the club". "Nah let's go get something to eat" . with that we peeled off and ended up at the *Low street Diner.* "So what's the new play. You bored so that means you need to change up the game". Randy looked at me eagerly awaiting my response. Randy has been my boy since we were kids, he was an aight looking dude but never had much game so a lot of the time he lived vicariously through me. I could see tonight would be one of those nights. "Randy my man I think i'm done playing all together. Women nowadays don't make you work for it because they are so busy thinking like men. When in reality they don't have the same emotional disconnect that is needed to separate sex and love". "Here you go putting that psychology degree to use, but nigga i'm not one of your patients i'm your boy. Give me the real". I shook my head at Randy "i'm serious. I think it's time I settled down. I'm a good looking dude, I have my own psychiatric practice, and i'm about to be thirty with no kids or std's. I'm like Jordan in his prime I rather go out on top than wait until i'm washed up". Randy stared at me for a second "you're serious". I nodded yes. Before we could finish our conversation our waitress finally arrived at our table "how can I help y'all". I gave Randy a look that said "*She ratchet as fuck*". "I'll have the Bacon egg and cheese omelette with hash browns and buttered toast" she smiled at me "somebody has a big appetite tonight, if you're still hungry in a hour give me a call I have something real tasty for you to try". With that she slipped a check slip onto the table with her number on it and walked off. She didn't even get Randy's order. "Yeah you getting out the game. I can't even get no food without chicks throwing their draws at you". We laughed when the waitress returned she had three plates full of food that we did not order. When she left the table she used her hand to mimic a phone and mouthed "call me". I giggled "see you got food. You're welcome". He laughed "she lucky I like everything she brought out". I joined in on his laughter and after we enjoyed our banquet of food I had Randy drop me off at my car Which was parked in a garage not to far from the club along with his car. It's also where we stash the getaway mobile until we are ready to go out on the town. I headed home thinking about my conversation I had with Randy at the diner. I was very serious about stepping back and settling down. I had been out here for years doing what seemed like the same kind of chicks. Most would play hard to get at first but eventually come back to the *smash pad*. Then there were the ones like Jessica aka the victim. The girl you meet out in a club or bar and they don't put up a fight at all but get mad when you treat them like exactly what it is, a hook up. My last serious girlfriend was in middle school because I learned at an early age women don't truly know what they want. Missy the last relationship I was in told me she wanted me to treat her like a lady. So that's what I did I gave her the complete gentlemens package. I opened doors, paid for all our dates, I even rubbed her feet. I did all that and then some to be the ultimate boyfriend and I never even got pass ass grabbing. She would tell me i'm a lady if you love me you'll wait, and what do I find my lady doing sucking dick behind the bleachers. Some lady. Ever since then I vowed to be single and have fun because women don't know what they want. High school is the beginning, that's when women set their sights on what they think is the man of their dreams. It's where you really start thinking about your future. I dated a lot in high school but I made it very clear I would not be tied down to one girl. I had an understanding that traveled with me until about age twenty five. That's when the ladies started to get real hostal hints the codes. Now that my thirtieth birthday is coming up I think it's time to retire the throne. A true pro knows when it's time to hang it up. Once I got in my house I ran for the shower. I needed to wash Jessica off of me before I called it a night. I had a few early sessions in the morning and it would be very unprofessional of me to show up late or hungover. The next morning I woke up bright and early feeling refreshed. I think removing the game from my mind acted as relief. I didn't think about who was in rotation or if I would find someone new to add to the team. I felt at ease with my decision to retire. Heading into the office my assistant Marcus greeted me with a cup of coffee and my schedule updates. My first patient Karen was a crazy white girl with a black girl body. Her problems were simple, her man wasn't putting it down at home and provided her with his credit cards to sooth her in his absence. I felt she had childhood issues she wouldn't address. When I asked her what she does when she gets loney she told me she masterbates and finds things to buy. She even admitted she only continues to come to me because it runs up his credit card bill. I set up at my desk preparing for her to enter. To my surprise she didn't come in alone. Walking behind her was a middle aged white man with a scowl on his face. "Good morning Damon, This is my husband Clarence. I hope you don't mind but he wanted to join us in our session today". I opened my mouth to respond but before I could get a word out Clarence cut me off. "You should be asking me if I mind you spending all of my money on this *doctor* who you call by his first name and I don't see anything wrong with you". "Mr. Hues if I may. Mental imbalance is not something that can be seen it's how the person feels on a daily basis. I allow all my patience to address me how they see fit it makes the process a lot easier. Now if you would like to join us today that would be great. Karen can express some things she has been feeling and we can show you some of the things we've been working on". Clarence wasn't the first disgruntled husband i've dealt with and if I stayed in business i'm sure he wouldn't be my last. "I am staying because I want to stay and I paid for the sessions not because you invited me let's be clear on that". "Understandable" for the next hour Karen expressed how she had been feeling neglected and Clarence had expressed his fears of losing her if he did not have any money. All in all a very successful session. I even got a few sections out of Clarence alone with some couple sessions in between. Karen had brought me more business than I bargained for but I was up for the challenge. After Karen came Sofie. Now Sofie is seeing me for OCD and mild depression. She is a soccer mom who never has any time to herself and needs her home and life to be perfect. With five kids and a lazy husband it amazes me how organized she is. "Hi Sophie have a seat I will be right with you". I watched from my desk as Sophie wiped down the seat and the table. "So Sophie how is this week going for you?". "It has been going great" she answered quickly as if she had been programed. Before I could address her denial she burst into tears. "Dr. Freemond I don't think I can do it anymore". Handing her the box of tissues I took my seat. "What can't you take anymore Sophie". She took a few tissues from the box and sobbed. "I feel alone all the time even though I am surrounded by people all day. I just left a PTA meeting and still I feel alone". "Sophie have you been doing the exercises we went over". She nodded yes. "Have you spoken with your husband about taking some of the burden off you?". Again she nodded her head yes. "What was his response". She looked up at me with the saddest eyes "he said if he wanted to do womens work he wouldn't have gotten married". I took a deep breath before I gave my advice. "Sophie do you remember what we talked about last week about putting yourself first sometimes". "Yes Dr. Freemond but what choice do I have. I married an old fashion ma. With five children I can't expect to have alone time all the time." I waited for her to finish defending her lack of boundaries and need to take care of herself as well as the others in her life."Sophie we both know you have responsibilities. We know that you are a homemaker and that you have to take care of your home but you also need to take care of you. I see that you have not set emotional boundaries with your husband as well. This concerns me. I would like for you to start setting aside thirty minutes out the day for yourself. Sophie began to shake nervously "Dr.freemond I have given you my schedule, I barely have time to come see you and you want me to take more time for what to waste. I can't do that Clive would be furious." Her protest was expected "I have a prescription for you. I am prescribing thirty minutes out of your day for anything but school events or anything that doesn't involve your household". I knew this would shock her system but I also knew that part of her disorder would force her to follow my prescription because it is ordered. "Dr. Freemond I... but..... What do I tell Clive?". "Tell him it's doctors orders. If he is willing to see you for not just his wife but his better half than you have a future. This prescription is for you to better yourself. If you're not ok your kids won't be ok". She pondered my words for a moment before taking the prescription from my hand. "Thank you Dr. Freemond". I paged Marcus over the intercom to let him know to order lunch for us. My last morning patient would be arriving in minutes and I wanted to be sure I could eat as soon as the session was over. My next session was with a new patient Ms. Mira Davies. Based on her file that Marcus created she is dealing with the loss of a child and fiance. She has been finding it hard to cope lately. Sounds like a case of depression but with all the problems that come with building a life and losing it there could be much more. "Dr. Freemond Ms. Davies is here". Marcus interrupted my thoughts. " Send her in Marcus, thank you". Reviewing her file one last time I moved to sit in the chair close to the couch. While I moved in walked the most stunning woman I had ever seen in my life. With a faint voice she reached out her hand. "Hi Dr. Freemond nice to meet you". I quickly composed myself "Nice to meet you Ms. Davies, please have a seat". She sat down in a slump. "How are you feeling today". I really didn't need to ask I could see she was emotionally spent. "I just am Dr. Freemond". "Can you tell me what brings you here today?". She looked at me with glassy eyes. "Well as I told your assistant I lost my child and fiance. We were in a car accident and I am the only one to survive". Nudging her to continue I nodded my head. "It was a regular day, we were heading to Josh's parents house for dinner. It took us a while to get in the car because Avery didn't want to get dressed. She wanted to stay home. I guess we should've listened. When we finally got on the road I insisted on driving". She sobbed a little I handed her a tissue and nudged her to finish her tragic story. " We drove for about twenty minutes before Avery began to fuss again. She kept saying she wanted to go home. Josh turned in his chair and calmed her down but she was very adamant on going home. We were waiting at a stop light so Josh decided to unbuckle his seatbelt and get in the back with Avery. I proceeded through the green light and before I knew it the car was spinning out of control. I woke up in the hospital a week later. I asked where Josh and Avery were quite a few times. All everyone kept telling me to do was calm down. My mother came and broke the news. Josh's parents had planned the funeral for both of them while I was in a coma. When I found out not only have I lost my child but my fiance as well I was devastated and angry. I missed the chance to give my family a proper burial and I survived. It wasn't fair. I had to spend another three weeks in the hospital for rehabilitation. While I worked on my health the world went on without me". I cut her off for a second "you mean it felt like the world went on without you". She just nodded and continued. "My sister and mother visited me everyday but I felt as if they were holding back on telling me things. I found out my almost mother in law blamed me for the accident and was actually protesting Josh's will because of it. The worst part about that situation was I had to find out from an agent who was investigating the crash. I wish my mom or my sister would have told me what was going on outside of those hospital walls". "I think they were just trying to protect you". Again she nodded and continued "I just think I would have handled it better hearing it from someone who knows me. After getting out of the hospital I had to go to court to fight my almost family. We spent all this time and energy fighting over a will that I never even wanted in the first place. All I wanted was my family back. I couldn't believe how heartless Macey was being. She demanded blood test results, psych evaluations and even went as far as to look into my childhood. Between the battle over the will and the court case against the driver of mack truck that crashed into us I was spent. I just want to move on from the grief. So that's why i'm here Dr. Freemond". I took a look at my notes before I responded. " Well there are plenty of things to work through and I can definitely help. I want to start you off with a session every week. What day would work for you?". "Thursdays would work best". I nodded "ok have my assistant set you up for the next four weeks and I will see you next week".

With lunch in my future my brain couldn't think of anything but food. "Marcus i'm ready for lunch". After eating I took a walk in the park to clear my mind a little and prepare for the rest of my day. For whatever reason I couldn't stop thinking about Mira. She had a ora about her that seemed to be draped with gloom. Heading back to the office Randy called me asking me to go to a mixer tonight. I really didn't want to go but he pleaded with me. "Come on man it's sophisticated women. You said you were done chasing women well with a mixer you don't have to chase they come to you". After listening to him whine a bit more I gave in. I decided I didn't have to participate I could have a few drinks and go support my boy. Once back in the office the rest of my day seemed to fly by like a blur. I headed home to get a good shower and prepare for the night. I spent about thirty minutes in the shower before I knew it Randy texted me letting know he was downstairs. He figured if he drove I wouldn't be able to ditch him. We dapped it up and headed out. The bar was very nice I saw a few that stood out from the pact but again I was here for support. "Man look at all these fine ass women in here. You picked the wrong time to get out the game". Randy looked happier than a fat kid in a candy store. "I picked the perfect time. Just try not to embarrass me or yourself. I will be the best wing man I can be but when it comes to actually snagging one of these ladies you're on your own". He laughed "My game is down i'm just glad I don't have to worry about you blocking". We headed to the bar to take our traditional shots before going on the prowl. "Hello can we get two shots of Patron". The bartender smiled placed two shots down and winked at me, looking down at my napkin I saw her number written down with a heart. "Let the games begin". Randy and I spent an hour mingling and collecting numbers. I hated to admit it but Randy was in rare form. He honestly didn't need me there, he had perfected his game and was working the room like a pro. I have to say I felt like a proud dad in the moment. I decided to let my man spread his wings I headed to the restroom to give him some space. Coming out the restroom I caught a glimpse of a woman who looked familiar. Heading back to the bar I saw the woman in full. It was Mira , her hair was different but it was definitely her. I battled with myself on weather to speak. I normally make it a point not to socialized with my patience outside of the office. Before I could decide weather to speak she was headed for the exit.

So I guess the powers that be saw fit to prevent an awkward moment this evening. I went on a search for Randy just to let him know I would leaving. I found him in a corner talking with a tall dark skin sister with a curly fro. "Excuse me I don't mean to interrupt. I'm out man". I said interrupting their conversation. "Excuse me for a second Shelly" he said to the modelesk woman. "Dog i'm killing it tonight, why you want to leave now?". I shook my head "i'm not tearing you away from all your fun I just wanted to let you know i'm out". He looked behind him at the woman as if weighing his options. "We can go I got enough numbers to tied me over for awhile". I looked over at the ebony queen standing waiting patiently for Randy to return, it wouldn't be right for me to rip him from what would turn out to be an epic night for him. "Nah man stay, play. I will be good". "You sure man I drove how you going to get home". Like clock work my phone alerted me my Lyft was outside. I smiled at him and took off. The week went on business as usual except for the fact I saw Mira around town more often. I made it a point not to speak and keep it professional. It was very tempting especially giving that fact that it was clear she wore a wig when we had our session to cover up her bob with pink highlights. Which I must say brings a different glow to her face. Thursday seemed to come faster than normal but I can't say I wasn't glad. I put out quite a few fires but Mira had my mind wondering. She had this solemn ora about her when she came to my office but when I see her out and about she has such a chipper vibe to her. I was eager to see which one showed up to my office today. I pulled out her file and reviewed my notes from our last session. Before I knew it Marcus was buzzing me informing me of her arrival. She walked in and I felt her energy. It was somber and not at all like the vibe I was getting seeing her around town. "Hi Dr. Freemond". "Ms. Davies". "Please call me Mira, I mean you are learning about my deepest thoughts and feelings I don't think using my first name isn't so far fetched". "Ok Mira it is". She took her seat on the couch and took a deep breath before she began. "I have been having nightmares, about the accident". I took note before I asked "how long have you been having these dreams. I'm mean nightmares". Her head hung so I couldn't see her expression. "To be honest they stopped after I left the hospital. Then I came here last week and just like that they were back". "Can you tell me about the nightmare?". She nodded "it always starts off the same we head out to go to Josh's parents house". She sniffled , I handed her the box of tissues. "The ending is always different. The first one there was a big storm and we crashed into a wall. I died but Avery and Josh survived. Last night Josh was driving and I got in the back seat with Avery". She dried her tears, "Do you die in all of them?". She nodded "all except one. Before I left the hospital I had one where Avery and I stayed home and Josh went alone. His mother called me asking me how far were we. I explained to her Avery was very upset so Josh would be coming alone. The next thing I know Avery is screaming daddy, daddy. I run into the living room and I see the car crash on the news then I woke up". "I know you probably figured this out but I feel like you are suffering from survivor's remorse, also known as guilt. You survived and you feel like you should have died with your family. How much sleep are you getting?". She nodded in agreement before answering. "Not much once I wake up i'm up. I think I got about four hours total all week". "How have you been doing socially, have you been spending time with your family any friends?". "The few friends I kept after collage live in other states. My sister tries to get me out of the house as much as possible but it's hard when just getting out of bed is a challenge". After making some notes I handed her a prescription. "I am prescribing you with 50mg of Trazodone. This is a low dose that should help your mood and help you get off to sleep". She looked at the paper before taking it from my hand. "I am not crazy."She said matter of factly. "I am not saying you are Mira, but you did tell me that you wanted my help is that not why you came here?". She nodded yes."Ok , that is all I am trying to do is help you. These are not pills for crazy people. These are pills to help you in your situation. I know it may be a little of putting but you have taken the first step by coming her and trust me those who don't are the crazy people". She smirked a bit. "Try them and if they don't work for you than we will find what will". She nodded as if finally understanding what I was trying to say. "I will see you next week. Be sure to see Marcus on your way out". With my last patient headed out the door I was ready to head home. I did some research and reached out to one of my colleagues about a support group for Mira. After a long day like today a beer and game highlights had my name written all over it. I checked my mail and retired to the couch for the rest of the evening. For the first time in a long time I couldn't sleep. I decided to head to the gym before work. After working out for about thirty minutes I spotted Mira putting in work on the bike. I must say she was definitely looking firm and right . I was very tempted to break the rules and approach her. I even got as close by lifting weights on the bench right in front of her. She looked right at me and before I made the decision to go up to her she was gone yet again. I guess she wasn't comfortable with hanging out outside of the office either. After a good workout I headed home to get ready for work. I was in a TGIF mood. It had been a long week and I needed to unwind this weekend. My boy Randy came to my office during lunch and told me about an event going on tonight. All I can say is right on time. From what he told me it's being thrown by the same people who threw the mixer we attended, but they partnered with an up and coming promoter who is into some different type of connections. We had to sign waivers before we could attend. The entire night is about making a connection without verbal communication. Stage one all the men are blindfolded and do a tasting of the ladies desert that best describe them. Stage two the fellas have to let the ladies smell there calone. The last stage is a dance of the hands. After the night ends we all put our numbers in our top three favorites baskets. I had a hard time picking three. After the dance of the hands it narrowed things down a lot easier. Now the kicker with receiving the numbers were we could not put our names on them. We would only be identified by our numbers provided to us at the event. My number of course was number one. I gave my number to number one, three and five. The rules were we could only exchange names when we went on our first date. Randy and I were still buzzing we decided to hit up our favorite diner and exchange notes on the event. "Man all those chicks felt bad up in there". I laughed "yeah considering we couldn't see them or hear their voice, hell they all could've been men for all we know". Randy shook his head addimitly no for one thing the woman who runs these things is an old client of mine she wouldn't do me like that. Two I felt necks and below looking for a bulge I wasn't getting played like that". We burst into laughter and went over the numbers we found in our baskets. To our surprise Randy had racked up all but two ladies ended up in his box. Ms. number three choose both of us. "Damn man I was hoping to get number five. That cheeseburger balmb was the shit". I shook my head "that shit was greasy, now number one killed it with the lamb. Number three was the only one who choose something sweet that's why I picked her. I guess she felt the same about my calone". Randy gave me a smirk "mine too". We laughed and ate then headed home. It looked like I had plans for the weekend. I decided to give Ms. number five a call and set up a brunch for that day. She needed a few tips on cooking with less grease but her body felt nice and she knew how to work her hips. "Hello may I speak to Ms. Number five". She seemed distracted "number five who is this". Her voice sounded familiar but I couldn't place it. " it's Mr. number one from last night". She giggled "oh this is she". We talked for about thirty minutes before I decided to invited her out to crestinis a local seafood breakfast spot. Weird combo but great food. On my way out the door to meet Ms. number five I got a call from Ms. number three. I told her I would meet up with her later for drinks. I needed to give myself enough time just in case brunch ran late. I told Ms. number five to meet me at the bar, I already had a table set up with a perfect view of the bar so I could get a good look at her when she walked in. That way I could still get my food and get out of there free and clear if she turned out to be not what I expected. I got to my table ten minutes before I told her to show up. I sat and waited for a woman to show up with a black and white dress on with the number five on it. She thought that was so funny that she had the perfect way for me to recognize her. After waiting for about twenty minutes I ordered a seafood omelet and a sparkling orange juice to go. The waiter brought me my food I saw Ms. number five walking to the bar. I decided to head over and give her a piece of my mind. When I got closer I saw her face and to my surprise I really did know her. Ms. number five was none other than Dana or Jessica whatever her name was. I made a dash for the exit. I got out just in time. When I got home I had three missed calls and two text messages. The last one told me what a loser I was and how I didn't know what I was missing. The joke was on her because I had been all up in that so I knew exactly what to look forward to. I hated to stand her up but another code 7 was not in the cards for me today. I prepared myself for for drinks at *4J Lounge*. Randy told me he was hooking up with her for dinner tomorrow so I decided to get it out of the way. I just wanted to see what I would be passing on. I could never dip where my boy would be dipping or trying to dip. Being that we would be meeting in a dim lit place Ms number three thought it would be cute to have three rose buds in her hair and a blue dress so I could spot her. I arrived ten minutes early to get the lay of the land. She walked in and I took notice immediately. She was bad long legs, nice hump on her back, butter skin, and this curly hair that just seemed to bounce. As she got closer she looked familiar but I couldn't place her. I brushed it off figuring I had just seen her around town or at the other event. On the other hand with eyes so big and bright that you would want to swim in I think I would have remembered her. I waved to her "Mr. number one" she said shaking my hand. I smiled "Ms. number three". She smiled "call me Missy". "I'm Damon". We had a few drinks and talked. She was a very cool chick. I felt like i've known her all my life. "So where did you grow up. I feel like I have known you forever". She asked talking the thoughts right out of my head. "I grew up in Nelson park, how about you". Her face lit up "me too". She giggled "well right on the other side in west pike, I went to Sheldon middle school and Franklin high". Just then it all came rushing back you me. Missy Mason the girl who broke my heart sat here before me not even knowing our connection. "Excuse for a moment I have to go to the little girls room". With that she left the bar and I was left to weigh my options. I wasn't sure how to play this. I mean I could just put her on blast then leave or I could smut her out like they did back in school. That just wasn't me. So many thoughts running through my head I knew that I had to make a move soon. I decided to pay the bill and leave. I told the bartender to give her a message. "Stay off your knees and you might find someone". "You really want me to say that man". I nodded and left. I called Randy and told him what wassup. He was a little disappointed but he hit it off with number four. I was happy for my man he was doing his thing out here. It was paying off. I was heading to bed when I received a text *I figured I would text you since I haven't received a call yet and the weekend is almost up. This is lady number one just in case you were wondering. I would like to put a voice with the name so if you are still up and still interested hit me up.* I smiled I loved women who were bold enough to make the first move. I called, couldn't let the moment pass. "Mr. number one I presume". I let out a chuckle "and that would make you lady number one". "Look we match already, so what took you so long to call". We talked until the sun came up exchanging everything but names and I have to say it felt good. I had felt a lot of emotions after seeing Missy tonight but lady number one help me forget all about that. We decided to meet up for dinner that night. Which worked out great because after talking all night I definitely needed the sleep. She texted me around noon to tell me how excited she was for our date tonight. I can't lie I was too. I took time to pick out the perfect suite. I finally settled on my black Kenneth Cole suit with red button down. I headed to *Big mama's.* It was an upscale soul food restaurant. I at the table with a single red rose in hand. I sat at the perfect viewpoint to see the door. After about five minutes I heard a sweet voice behind me. "Is that rose for me mr. number one". I was pleasantly surprised that she had not only beat me to the restaurant but got the drop on me. I turned around and was even more shocked. "Mira".

www.ingramcontent.com/pod-product-compliance
Lightning Source LLC
Chambersburg PA
CBHW061301040426
42444CB00010B/2456